EUCLID

THE MAN WHO INVENTED GEOMETRY

Shoo Rayner

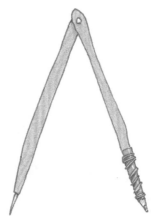

First Published 2012

Revised edition
© 2017 Shoo Rayner

www.shoorayner.com

ISBN 978-1-908944-36-8

CHAPTER 1

A long, long, long, long time ago, about 2300 years ago, to be a little more precise, there lived a man in Ancient Greece called Euclid.

He looked nothing like this drawing - this is just an idea of how he might have looked.

Euclid was one cool Ancient Greek!

Over a thousand years after Euclid died, someone else thought he might have looked like this...

Euclid wrote the first great book on geometry. It must have been a really good book, because schools were still using it to teach geometry well into the 20th century.

Euclid's book was called Euclid's Elements

a •

All the best ideas are simple and brilliant and Euclid had a really simple and brilliant idea!

Euclid thought he would explain stuff by starting at the very beginning.

He would find something very simple that everyone could agree with. Then he would build on that simple idea.

Euclid decided that a simple point - a fixed position in space - was a good place to start.

You can think of a point as if it were a cross on a map that shows where treasure has been buried.

X marks the spot!

Euclid explained this to his friends and they all said, "What a simple and brilliant idea. We get the point!"

"Now," said Euclid, "let's make another point. We'll call the first point a and the second point b."

a •   • b

"Okay," said everyone. "We're happy with that."

"Now, let's connect the two points together with a line," said Euclid.

a •————————————• b

"The shortest distance between the two points is called a SEGMENT of a line, but I'm just going to call it a LINE."

"A line is a thing that has length but no width or height," said Euclid ."A segment is a part of a line with a point at each end."

"Yes!" Everyone said. "We understand."

"I'm going to call this simple idea an Axiom," said Euclid. "An Axiom is something everyone can agree with, a starting point from which we can begin to work out other stuff."

"That is so cool!" said Euclid's friends. "Have you got any more great ideas like that?"

"Lots" said Euclid, "but that's enough for today. Tomorrow I'll show you what happens if we have three points instead of two."

"Cool!" said his friends.

Then they all drew diagrams in the sand. Some drew wiggly lines... some drew zig zags, some wrote their names.

But whatever they did, they had to agree that the shortest distance between two points was made by a straight and simple segment of a line.

Axiom

An axiom is something that everyone agrees is obvious and true.

You can use the axiom you have already proved as a starting point to try out new ideas and theories.

CHAPTER TWO

"Geometry is all about relationships," said Euclid.

"Ooh!" said
Euclid's friends,

"Euclid's got
a girlfriend!"

"Not that kind
of relationship!"
Euclid sighed.

Euclid drew two lines exactly the same length
and made them exactly the same distance apart.

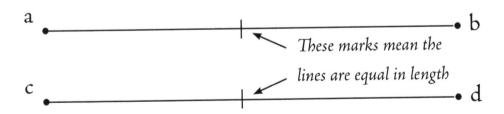

*These marks mean the
lines are equal in length*

"These lines are exactly the same length as each
other," Euclid said. "That makes them equal and that's
a relationship - the lines are equal to each other!"

"If you carry on drawing these lines in the same direction for ever and ever," Euclid explained, "the lines will never, ever meet, because they will always be the same distance apart."

PARALLEL

These marks mean the lines are parallel

"We will call them PARALLEL lines.
Being parallel to each other is another relationship."

"Ah!" said Euclid's friends. "But what happens if the lines are not always the same distance apart?"

"If you carry on drawing lines that are not always the same distance apart, they will eventually meet - like this," said Euclid.

This is the point where the lines converge

Converging

"Now the lines have a new relationship. Because they are eventually going to meet or CONVERGE, we'll call them CONVERGING lines."

Then Euclid drew two equal lines which were joined together at one end.

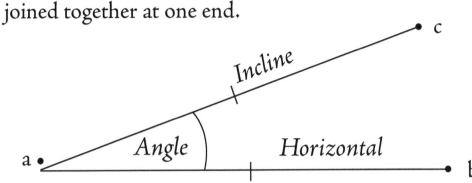

"These lines are still equal in length," said Euclid, "but they now have a new relationship."

"One is kind of flat like the horizon. We can call that a HORIZONTAL line. The other line is an INCLINE. It looks like it's going up, like a hill."

"We can call the steepness of the hill, or the amount of hillyness, the ANGLE between the two

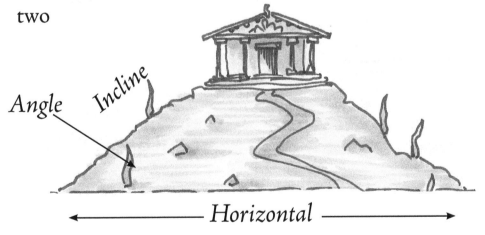

"That's really neat!" said Euclid's friends, or something like that.

"But that's not all," said Euclid. "We now have three points a, b and c.

The two lines are connected at a. We could join the two other points, b and c, with a new line."

"Amazing!" said Euclid's friends.

"Now each line has a relationship with another line, and those relationships are angles. So we have three points and three lines and three angles. I think we should call this new shape a *Threeangle!*"

A THREE ANGLE!

"Oh!" Euclid's friends sounded disappointed.

"For some reason, that just doesn't sound right," they said. "Remember we are Ancient Greeks."

"How about Triangle?" Euclid suggested.

"Oh yes!" Euclid's friends cheered. "That sounds much better."

"Okay!" Euclid said, triumphantly. "A shape with three points and three lines and three angles is called a TRIANGLE."

Okay!
A Triangle!

CHAPTER THREE

"If you read the last chapter about angles," said Euclid, "you will remember that two lines which are joined at the same point will have an angle between them unless they are on top of each other."

"Okay…" said Euclid's friends. They wondered where Euclid was going with this idea.

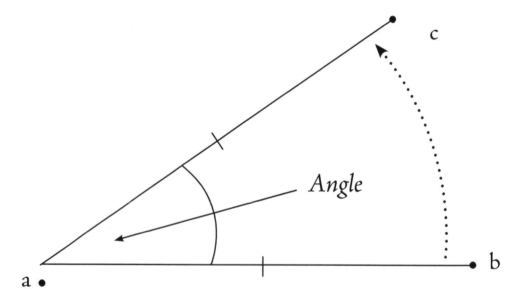

"If you start with both lines completely horizontal and on top of each other, and then begin raising one of the lines at one end, you will create a sharp, pointy angle where they are connected at a.

We shall call this an ACUTE ANGLE," said Euclid.

"Cute!" cheered Euclid's friends.

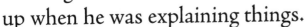

"No! Not cute!" Euclid said, firmly. "Acute!"

"Okay!" Euclid's friends laughed. They did enjoy winding Euclid up when he was explaining things.

"Keep raising the line till it gets to the very top, just before it goes over to the other side," said Euclid. "We shall call this a RIGHT ANGLE and and we'll draw a little square at the bottom to let everyone know."

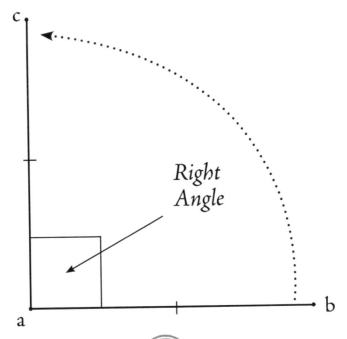

Right Angle

"Right!" said Euclid's friends. Euclid gave them a look.

RIGHT!

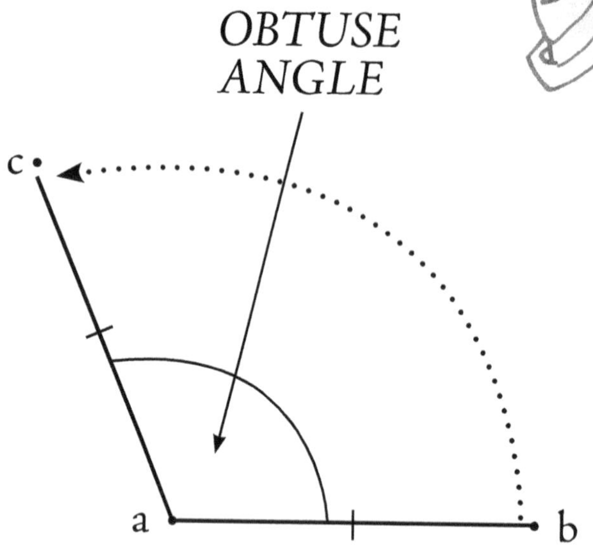

OBTUSE ANGLE

c

a   b

"If you carry on rotating the line, the angle won't be so pointy any more," said Euclid. "We will call this an OBTUSE ANGLE."

"The angle gets more and more obtuse until both lines are horizontal, then the two lines make one line, which is twice as long as when they started."

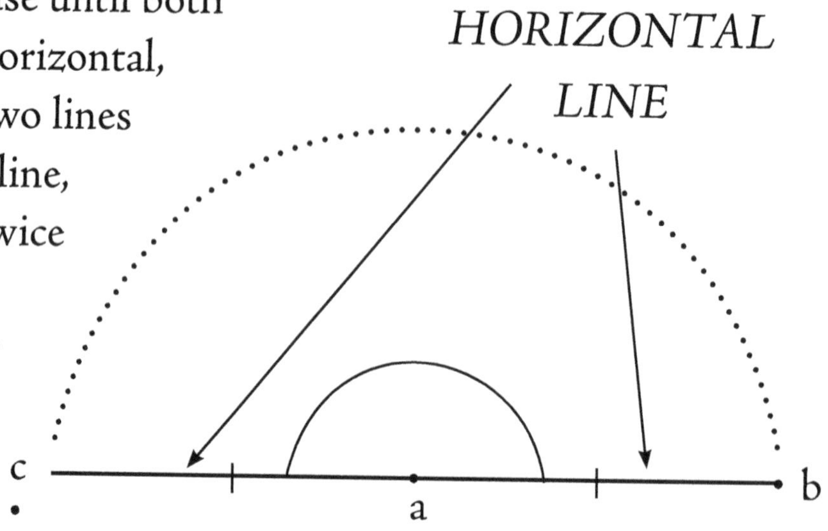

HORIZONTAL LINE

c   a   b

"The line can rotate all the way around until it comes back to where it started," Euclid explained.

"Now - look what happens when we follow the journey made by the point at the other end of the line."

Euclid's friends watched in amazement as Euclid drew the shape.

"It's a CIRCLE !" they exclaimed.

"Well done!" said Euclid, glad that his friends had been paying attention. "Do you remember I said that geometry was all about relationships? Well the lines have a special relationship to the circle."

"The line that goes from the middle of the circle to the outside is called the RADIUS."

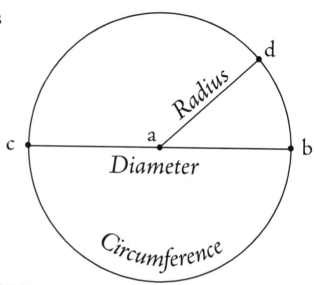

"And the line that goes across, and right through the centre point, is called the... DIAMETER."

"What's the outside called?" asked Euclid's friends.

"Erm... the CIRCUMFERENCE!" said Euclid, saying the first thing that came into his head that sounded circley.

"That's amazing!" said Euclid's friends.

"It is!" Euclid agreed.

CHAPTER FOUR

"With all these angles and right angles," said Euclid's friends. "Is there some way we can measure them?"

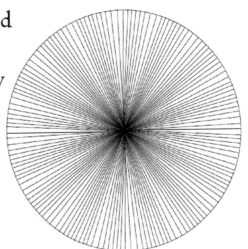

"Ahh!" Euclid beamed. "That's a really good question. Look at this circle."

"If you put all the angles inside it together, they add up to 360 measuring thingy-bits that we will call DEGREES." (Euclid really was good at thinking up names for things.)

Euclid's friends looked baffled. "You just made that up!" they grumbled.

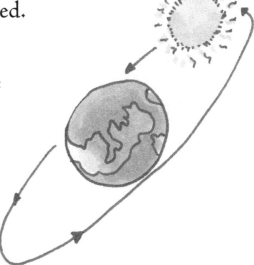

"No, look!" said Euclid. "Here is Earth at the centre of the Universe. Every year the sun goes round the Earth 360 times. That's where the number of degrees comes from."

(In those days they didn't know that it's the other way around, and the Earth really goes around the Sun!)

"But there are 365 days in the year!" Euclid's friends protested.

365!

"Well, strictly speaking, you're right," said Euclid, "but 360 is a much better number. 360 can be divided by a whole bunch of numbers which makes it really easy to work with."

$360 \div 2 = 180$	$360 \div 9 = 40$
$360 \div 3 = 120$	$360 \div 10 = 36$
$360 \div 4 = 90$	$360 \div 12 = 30$
$360 \div 5 = 72$	$360 \div 15 = 24$
$360 \div 6 = 60$	$360 \div 18 = 20$
$360 \div 8 = 45$	$360 \div 20 = 18$

Don't you see how useful that is?

Euclid's friends looked baffled.

"This is where it starts to get interesting," Euclid beamed. "Half a circle has 180 degrees in it, so a quarter of a circle has 90 degrees, because 90 x 2 =180."

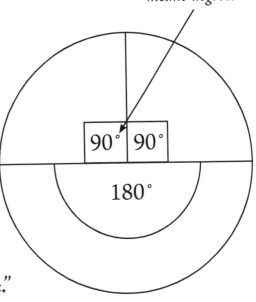

The little circle after the number means degrees

"Okay…" said Euclid's friends. "That makes sense."

"Do you remember how we made two lines of equal length into a right angle?" Euclid asked.

"Errr… yes!" mumbled Euclid's friends, who were beginning to feel a bit dizzy with all the numbers.

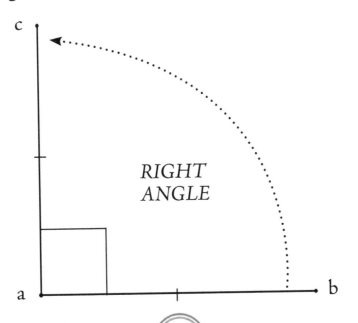

RIGHT ANGLE

"You can do the same thing and join another line of equal length at the point b and rotate it up to the top at point d, making a new right angle." said Euclid.

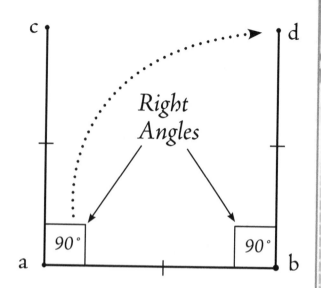

"And then you can draw a line across the top to join the two remaining points, c and d. Now you get a new shape with four right-angled corners."

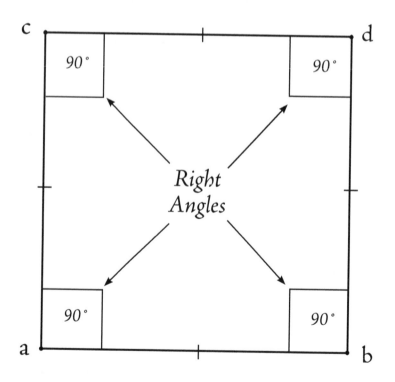

"That is so cool!" said Euclid's friends. It looks sort of…"

"SQUARE is the word you are looking for," said Euclid.

When all the lines are of equal length and at ninety degrees to each other, we call it a SQUARE!

CHAPTER FIVE

"We really love triangles," said Euclid's friends, "but we can't help noticing that they don't all look the same."

"Well spotted!" said Euclid. "The shape of a triangle depends on the length of its lines and the size of its angles."

"The most simple triangle has everything equal - its sides and angles are all the same. We call this shape an EQUILATERAL TRIANGLE."

Euclid's friends nodded their heads wisely.

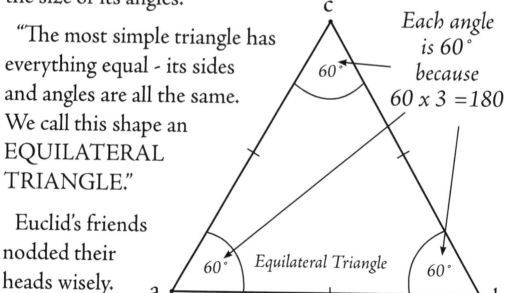

Each angle is 60° because 60 x 3 = 180

Equilateral Triangle

"If we change the length of just one line, we now have two lines of equal length and two angles the same."

"This we call an ISOSCELES TRIANGLE," said Euclid

"Iced Sausages?" Euclid's friends gasped in disbelief!

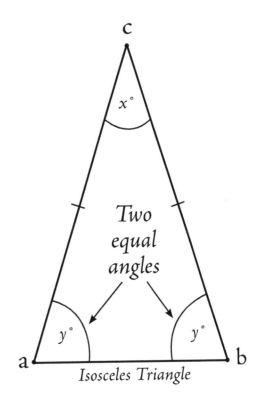

Two equal angles

Isosceles Triangle

"I-soss-ill-ees!" Euclid said, very slowly. "Isosceles!"

I-soss-ill-ees!

Euclid was really good at thinking up names for things, but some of the words he chose were quite hard to say and some were even harder to spell!

"If all the sides of a triangle are different," said Euclid, "then so must be all the angles.
We call a triangle with different length sides a SCALENE TRIANGLE."

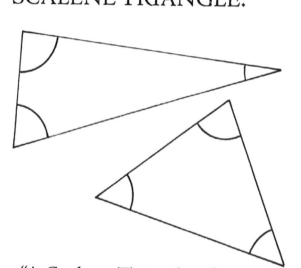

Three acute angles

"A Scalene Triangle…" Euclid's friends repeated. "Is that it for triangles then?"

"Not quite," said Euclid. There are three different types of Scalene Triangle.

If all the angles in the triangle are acute - that is that they are all smaller than 90° - then it's called an ACUTE SCALENE TRIANGLE!"

"Oh! Cute!" smiled one of Euclid's friends.

"You did that joke in Chapter Three," Euclid frowned, " and it wasn't funny then!"

CUTE!

"Sorreee!" Euclid's friend giggled. He thought it was a really funny joke !

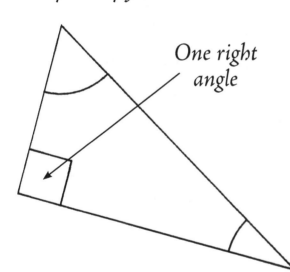

One right angle

"If a triangle has one right angle, then it is called a RIGHT-ANGLED SCALENE TRIANGLE," said Euclid.

"Oh right!" Euclid's friends whooped.

"And finally…," Euclid said firmly, "a triangle with one obtuse angle, that is to say an angle that is greater than 90°, is called…"

"An OBTUSE SCALENE TRIANGLE!" Euclid's friends cheered.

One obtuse angle

Euclid smiled. "I think you're finally getting the hang of all this geometry stuff."

"What about squares?" Euclid's friends asked. "Are there different types of square too?"

"There is only one type of square and that is a square one," said Euclid. "A square has four right-angled corners and four lines of equal length."

"There are all sorts of four-sided shapes" said Euclid, "but I'll tell you about them in the next chapter. All this talk of sausages has made me hungry!"

CHAPTER SIX

"Four-sided shapes are called QUADRILATERALS," said Euclid. "Quad means four and lateral means side, so quadrilateral means a four-sided shape."

"If we make a square wider or taller, we get a new shape called a RECTANGLE."

"A rectangle can be tall or wide or thin or flat but it must still always have four right angles, the same as the square."

"Ahh!" Euclid's friends looked happy again.

"As well as having four right angles, a rectangle has two pairs of lines that are both parallel and equal to each other in length."

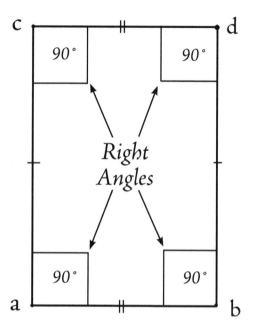

"Right!" said Euclid's friends.

"You're repeating your jokes again!" Euclid sighed.

"Well, there aren't many jokes in Geometry," Euclid's friends complained.

"Without Geometry," Euclid said, mysteriously, "life would be pointless!"

"That's a good one!" Euclid's friends laughed.

"Now, if we kind of push the top of a square over to one side a bit, the corner angles change. We get two pairs of equal angles, but the lines are all still the same length. We'll call this a RHOMBUS."

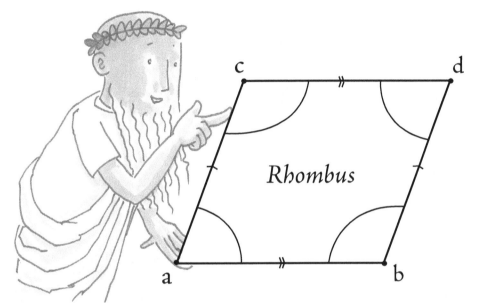

Rhombus

"We can do the same thing with a rectangle, but this time the new shape is called a PARALLELOGRAM.

The opposite sides are still parallel. We no longer have any right angles but two pairs of new angles."

"Cool!" said Euclid's friends.

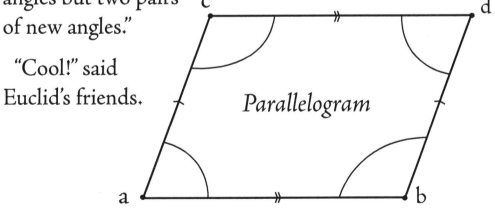

Parallelogram

"If we change the lengths of one of the lines, we get something that looks like a swing or a flying trapeze," said Euclid. "We'll call it a TRAPEZIUM, although they'll call it different things in different countries in the future."

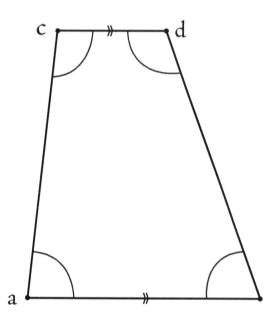

"A Trapezium has only one pair of parallel lines."

"Any other shape that has four sides that are not equal in length, and four angles that are not equal either, is called an IRREGULAR QUADRILATERAL," said Euclid.

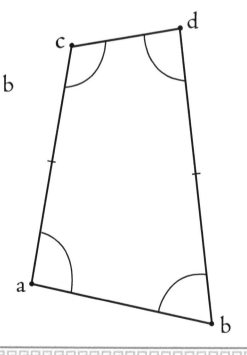

"When there are two pairs of equal angles and two opposite lines are of equal length, it looks like an isoceles triangle with the top knocked off. We call this an ISOCELES TRAPEZIUM."

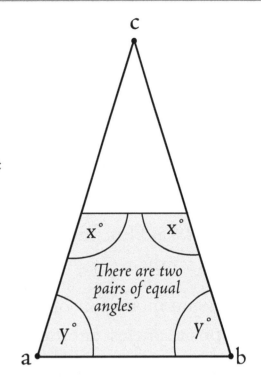

There are two pairs of equal angles

"Sausages again!" Euclid's friends cheered.

"You did that joke in the last chapter too!" Euclid sighed.

"Sorreeee!" said Euclid's friends.

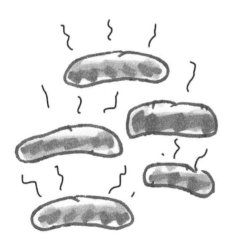

"Are there any more quadrilaterals?"

"Well, if you turn a rhombus on it's side, you get a DIAMOND, but it's actually still the same shape."

"And everything else, that has no parallel lines is just a common every-day irregular quadrilateral... except... if two lines are equal, and the other two lines are equal but of a different length..."

"Yes?" said Euclid's friends, expectantly.

"... and if one pair of opposite angles are the same..."

"Yes?" said Euclid's friends, desperate to know more.

"Then we get a shape called..."

"Yes?" said Euclid's friends, who were besides themselves by now.

"Then we get a shape called... a kite!" said Euclid.

Chapter Seven

"We've done triangles and squares," said Euclid's friends. "Are there any more shapes? What happens if you add more points? Do you get new shapes?"

"We do," said Euclid, who was pleased that his friends were getting interested in Geometry now.

"But first I'm going to show you how to cut things in half."

"Do you want to borrow my penknife?" asked one of Euclid's friends.

"No, thanks," said Euclid.

"All we need is a compass and a ruler." Euclid's friend looked baffled.

"Set the compass to the same width as the line we want to cut in half."

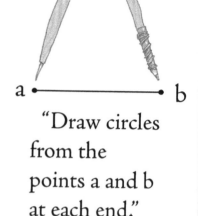

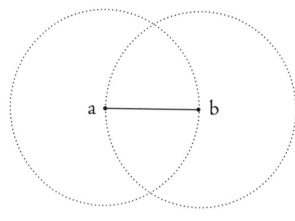

"Draw circles from the points a and b at each end."

"Then draw a line through the points where the circles cross each other."

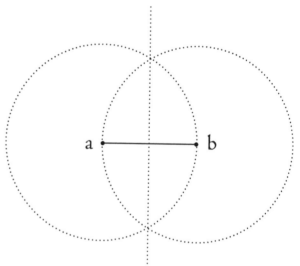

"That's amazing!" Euclid's friends gasped!

"It is," Euclid smiled. "The first line has been BISECTED."

"Bi means two and Sect is short for Section, so Bisect means to cut into two equal sections," Euclid explained.

"The new line is PERPENDICULAR to the original line, which is another way to say they are at right angles to each other."

"Fantastic!" cheered Euclid's friends.

"You can do the same with angles," said Euclid.

Lines that are at right angles to each other are called perpendicular

c

90°

a

b

d

"From the sharp point of the angle at a, draw an arc, so it crosses both lines at d and e."

c

a

b

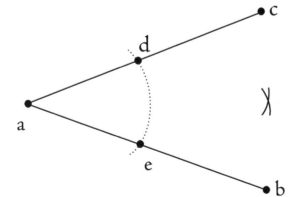

c

d

a

e

b

"Draw two arcs from the points where the first arc crosses the lines at d and e."

"Then draw a line through the points where the arcs cross each other at f and the point of the angle a. Now the angle has been BISECTED too!"

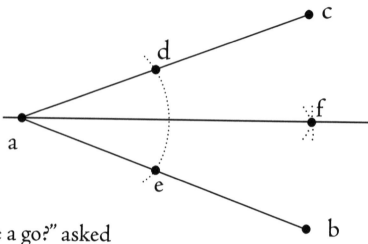

"Can we have a go?" asked Euclid's friends, enthusiastically.

"You can," said Euclid.

"Just be careful not to stab yourselves with the sharp point of the compass!"

"We will be very careful!" said Euclid's friends.

Chapter Eight

"Shapes with many sides are called POLYGONS," said Euclid. "POLY means many and GON means angle, so polygons have many sides and many angles."

"What about the parrots?" asked Euclid's friends.

"Parrots?" enquired Euclid, testily. "What parrots?"

"You know
- Pretty Polly -
- Polly gone!"
laughed Euclid'sfriends.

Euclid cleared his throat noisily and continued.

"Triangles and squares are polygons," said Euclid, "but we usually call them triangles and squares."

"When all the sides of a polygon are equal in length, we call the shape an EQULILATERAL POLYGON."

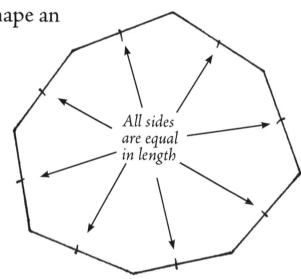

All sides are equal in length

"That's neat," said Euclid's friends.

"And when a polygon's sides and angles are all equal, we call it a REGULAR POLYGON."

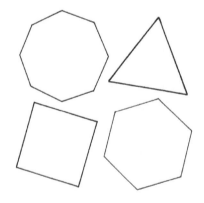

"That's very neat," said Euclid's friends.

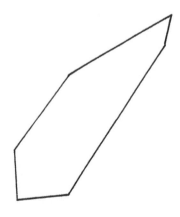

"When the sides and angles of a polygon are not equal, we call it an IRREGULAR POLYGON." Euclid explained.

"Oh, that's not so neat," said Euclid's friends.

"If one or more of the angles is greater than 180°," said Euclid, "the shape will look as if it has had a bite taken out of it. We call this kind of shape CONCAVE."

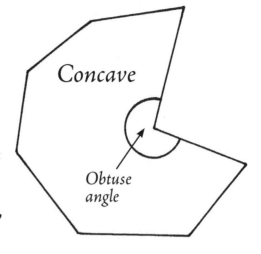

Concave

Obtuse angle

"Oh, that's really messy!" Euclid's friends groaned.

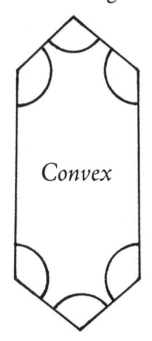

Convex

"But, if all the angles are less than 180°, then the shape is called CONVEX." said Euclid.

"Oh, but we like them cute!" said one of Euclid's friends.

CUTE!

Euclid gave his friends a long, cold stare!

"And we like them convex and concave too!" Euclid's friend smiled, cheesily.

CHAPTER NINE

"A square can fit perfectly inside a circle," said Euclid.

"Oh that's very neat!" said Euclid's friends.

"Well, look what happens if we bisect the sides of the square."

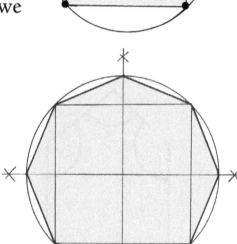

"When we connect the points where the lines intersect the circle, we get a new regular shape with eight sides."

"It's called an OCTAGON."

"An octopus!" cheered Euclid's friends.

Euclid ignored his friends. He was getting tired of their silly jokes.

"Try this…" said Euclid. "Bisect a circle by drawing a line through it's centre."

"Then, with the same radius as the circle, draw two arcs from the points where the line crosses the circumference at a and b."

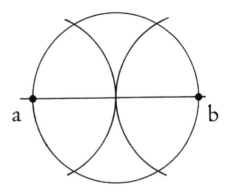

"Look - the circumference is now cut into six equal arcs. Join the six intersecting points and we get a regular HEXAGON, or six-sided polygon," said Euclid.

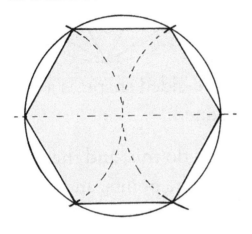

"That's really neat!" said Euclid's friends.

"Join all the points to the centre and you get six, smaller equilateral triangles in a pattern."

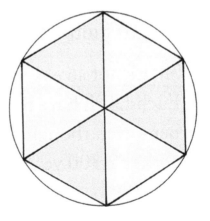

"Join just three points of the hexagon and you get one equilateral triangle," said Euclid.

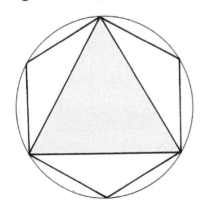

"Or join all the points to each other with lines and you get the shape of a six-sided star which is called a HEXAGRAM."

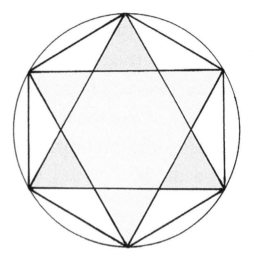

"That's beautiful!" cheered Euclid's friends.

"Now… a PENTAGON, or five-sided shape, is a bit more complicated," Euclid explained.

"You do this, then that, then you do this, and then you do that, and then you join up the points, and there you are, a Pentagon."

"That was a bit fast," said Euclid's friends. "We couldn't quite see how you did that!"

"Well, it's not so easy to construct a pentagon," said Euclid, "I'll have to do a video and put it on the internet - even though the internet won't be invented for another 2,300 years!"

find the link at
www.shoorayner.com/euclid

"Can you make stars and triangles with a pentagon too?" asked Euclid's friends.

"You can make a five-sided star called a PENTAGRAM," said Euclid.

"Wow!" said Euclid's friends.

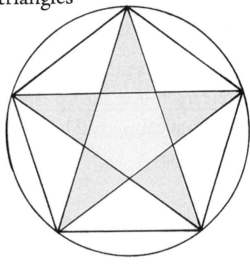

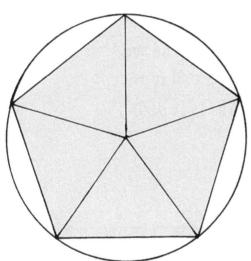

"And you can make five isoceles triangles."

Euclid's friends bit their tongues and said nothing about sausages.

"A HEPTAGON, or seven-sided polygon is almost impossible to construct," said Euclid. "So I'm not going to try! And there are NONAGONS and DECAGONS and HENDECAGONS and DODECAGONS - add a sausage and you get a HOT-DOG-ON!"

"And ON-AND-ON-AND-ON!" laughed Euclid's friends.

"Can you have as many sides as you like in a polygon?" asked Euclid's friends?

"You can," said Euclid. "In fact you could say the circle itself is made up from an infinite number of points connected by an infinite number of very short lines."

"I suppose we could call it an INFINIGON!"

CHAPTER 10

"Now," said Euclid," to finish up, I'm going to show you a neat thing about the angles in Polygons."

"Each time you add a new point to a shape you are really adding a triangle."

"Huh!?" Euclid's friends were confused.

"A Rectangle is made from two triangles."

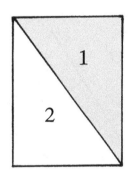

"A Pentagon is made from three triangles."

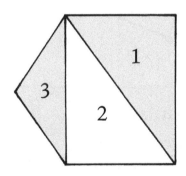

"A Hexagon is made from four triangles."

"Okay," said Euclid's friends.

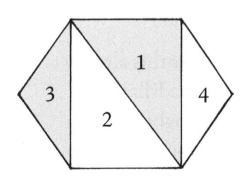

"Let's start with a triangle and work from there," said Euclid.

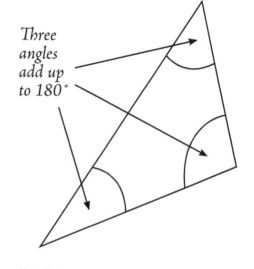

Three angles add up to 180°

"A triangle has three points, three lines connecting them and three angles, which always add up to 180°."

"Add a point outside the triangle and join it to the nearest corners, and you get a four-sided shape, or quadrilateral."

"Okay…" said Euclid's friends, who were following this lesson very carefully.

"The quadrilateral is made of two triangles. That means its angles add up to 360°."

"We knew this already because quadrilaterals have four right angles of 90°, which add up to 360° as well."

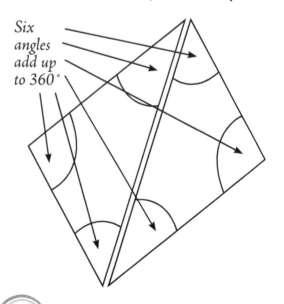

Six angles add up to 360°

"Add a new point and connect it to the quadrilateral, and you get a new five-sided shape or PENTAGON."

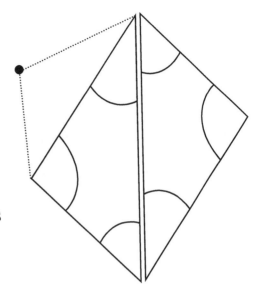

"There are three triangles in a Pentagon so the angles must add up to…?" Euclid let his friends work it out.

"Um…! Errr…!" Euclid's friends nearly ran out of fingers to count on.

"540°!" they said, together.

Three triangles
180° + 180° + 180°
add up to 540°

"Well done!" Euclid smiled.

"And we can show it's true another way…" he said.

"Remember how we made a Pentagon inside a circle?" Euclid asked.

"We remember," said Euclid's friends.

"When we connect the points of the Pentagon to the centre of the circle we get five Isosceles Triangles." said Euclid.

"Five sausages!" cheered Euclid's friends.

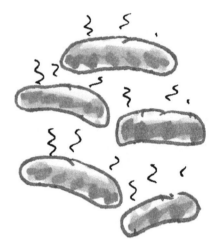

"You really have run out of jokes, haven't you?" said Euclid.

"Sorreeee!" Euclid's friends groaned.

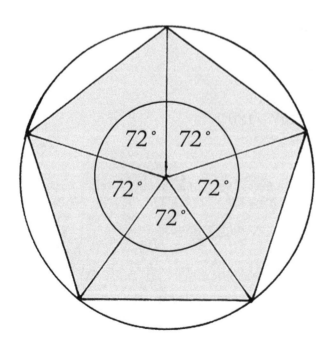

"We know that there are 360° around the centre point of a circle. Divide 360 by 5 and we get 72° for all the centre angles of the triangles." Euclid explained.

"Well," said Euclid. "There are 180° in each triangle. 180° minus 72° leaves 108° for the other two angles in each triangle."

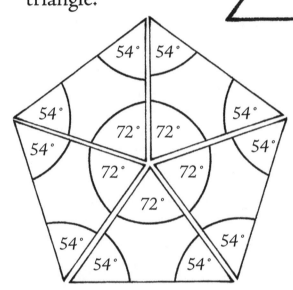

"As they are isoceles triangles, the other angles are equal, so they add up to a half of 108°, which is 54°. So each angle is 54°."

"Now we have ten angles altogether in the pentagon, each angle is 54°, so what does that add up to?"

Euclid's friends could multiply by ten easily.

"Add a zero on the end and you get 540°!" they cheered. "Just the same as adding up the three triangles like we did before!"

540!

"Well done!" said Euclid. "I really think you're getting the hang of geometry now."

"Does this geometry stuff work with boxes and pyramids and things like that?" asked Euclid's friends.

"It does," said Euclid. "But maybe we will do that another day."

"Oh!" Euclid's friends were sad. "Do you know any more geometry jokes?"

"Yes," said Euclid.

"Why did the obtuse angle go out in the midday sun?"

"We don't know!" said Euclid's friends. "Why did the obtuse angle go out in the midday sun?"

"Because it was over 90 degrees in the shade!" Said Euclid.

MORE OF EUCLID'S FAVOURITE GEOMETRY JOKES

What do you get when you cross a pebble with a sphere?

Rock and Roll!

What did one geometry book say to the other?

Don't bother me I've got my own problems!

Who invented the Round Table?

Sir Cumference!

Why was the geometry teacher limping?

Because she sprained her angle!

What did the square say to the circle?

"I haven't I seen you round here lately!"

If you have enjoyed this book and would like to know more about Euclid and his inventions,
go to Shoo Rayner's website at:

www.shoorayner.com/euclid

There you can discover more about euclid and geometry and even learn to draw Euclid himself, with how-to-draw videos from Shoo's award-winning YouTube Channels.

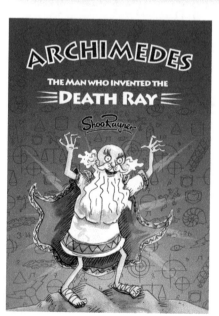

If you really like this book, then you may also like **Archimedes, *The Man Who Invented The Death Ray*.**

Archimedes was also a brilliant Mathamatical Mega-Mind .

Lightning Source UK Ltd.
Milton Keynes UK
UKHW031132310322
400890UK00006B/486